T0198596

Good Old Days

Memories With My Family And Great Friends

LARRY SELIG

GOOD OLD DAYS
MEMORIES WITH MY FAMILY AND GREAT FRIENDS

iUniverse books may be ordered through booksellers or by contacting:

iUniverse
1663 Liberty Drive
Bloomington, IN 47403
www.iuniverse.com
844-349-9409

ISBN: 978-1-6632-4694-3 (sc)
ISBN: 978-1-6632-4696-7 (e)

Print information available on the last page.

iUniverse rev. date: 10/19/2022

my email seliglarry1@gmail.com year 2019 Oct Wed second is when i started the book this is a true story my very words, the book goes way back in history, go way back in the 60s i would say or 70s, cause i was born Feb 13th 1957, and i started working when i was about 13 or 14, i used to help Daddy peal wood, the oh bark off the wood i remember that.

CHAPTER 1

All About My Family and the Friends I Know and It was All Love

Well i am in my bedroom tonight, 5 after 7PM, at my desk, i look out my bedroom window. and see the pretty wonderful trees. Oh it is a still night and i see the pretty bright stars shine, wonderful to me. Well my brother David lives right across on the other lane from me, just a 5 min walk to go over and talk to him. Oh we chat about things, he likes cars, he gets wonderful great looking ones. Well my bike and computer he can fix them, and he does for me. Well i am so glad i have a brother like that, he can fix things no matter what it is. Well my other brother Ronnie lives down the road a bit more, i don't see him a lot, but he is not that far that i can't go see him, and my sister Shirley lives down the road pass Ronnie's, so my family they are close to go see. Well i have another sister Lois, she lives up the mountain, that i don't get there that much anymore, i have no way there really. Well be to far on a paddle bike, i am getting older i am 62 of age now, but i get a drive by friends to get up, my birthdate Feb 13th that is my birthday, that is not to far off from now. Well my older brother Everett he got sick and passed in 200,00 and 6 i believe, and he was 60 something and i had another older sister Gloria, she passed around 40 i think and she was wonderful, she would help anyone she could, and she used to go too church me i go to church if not working, and i can get there, it is just up the road aways. Well i do like church. Well there was another brother Allen, well he got hit by a moving car and got killed, i was there when it all happen i was about 15 or 16, it took a lot out of me but got through it. Well my sister Gloria's girl Lori, we had fun in the good ol days, cause i used to live with them i would always all Lori Lor a lot, and when she lost control of her car one day, it wasn't funny but in away it was, cause we would say Lori what are you trying to do kill your self, her mother and me we laughed a bit, the way she was getting out of the car, and Lori looking in at us, we were laughing and saying well what was you trying to do, she said i missed that darn corner, and we are sorry about laughing, and we said be careful girl, and i think Lori was crying a bit, and her mom Gloria said come here we love you but just be careful okay, and Lori said yes she will, and things got better, and she never got hurt that was the main thing.

Chapter 2

More About Family and Friends

Oct 2019, Monday 14th

Well me and my family, i remember we all would get together, and we would sing songs, we would always sing and i play guitar, and some brothers to would play guitar. Well they were good we would dance, we would get up and dance, having a great time. Oh it was all good fun, and i live alone, and i am happy, i get out to see friends and that i get around. Well if i go before the rest of the family, i hope one of them would carry this out, it could mean something to them, but i hope they will take this to the top if something happens to me. Well i hope i can get this done myself, then i know it is done. I know it is hard to get my family in on this, they don't know they are in the book, but don't think they would mind, but i know they would read what i got down in this book. Well if the book gets out, they would have to buy one, well not really, i would give them one, i know they would like that too. Well i was working tonight just got home a while, i was cleaning the floors, i been cleaning for along time now, i have cleaned a lot of stores at Greenwood Mall, Giant Tiger, up in New Minas. Oh i did help in Choppers i been around with a friend his name Joey he has learned me a lot i couldn't use a broom right Joey taught me he has a woman named Amanda they are great friends, still are even that i don't do work with him now after i had a heart a tack. Well but he knew i have done good work, and i worked in the woods with my brothers, just piling wood but not to much with a power saw, i wasn't that good with one. I never used them that much because they thought i may cut myself, or jam the power saw in a tree and i have, with my brother Ronnie there. Oh he said well enough of that laugh out loud, and i have worked with my other brother David but same thing, i jammed the saw, so i thought to stick it out to piling wood. Well i was best of doing that, and done a great job, they said i was a great pilier, that i do wonderful work. Well this is 2020 month April 9th, and this Coronavirus is all over the world, it is bad we are to stay in, and go out to get our food and right back home again, not looking good yet. So if i get sick and die well this book won't get out, but I hope things go in flying colors. Oh Jesus keeps me alive through this, but hard to say, everything pretty much lockdown all over, but i do a lot of praying i can do, while i am still here and hope to be, to get this book out. People have fear, don't know what to do, bills not getting paid, and scared, well it is bad. Oh i pray for them to have faith in Jesus, go to Jesus i am not that worked up, i know Jesus works within me i believe that, and i do get strong feelings, i let my sister Shirley know, cause right now she is the only one that believes me, i talk to rest of the family but seems like they are not getting it, but it is true, it says in a song but though none go with me but i will still follow, well God Bless them, i will still pray and keep going and hope to see them in heaven, and my friends Joey and Amanda they were always good to me they still are i see Amanda working in the Greenwood Mall, i have been going there a lot i still do when i can me and Joey we worked together a lot, we worked to a lot of stores digby up in New Minas, and to the theater where you watch movies in New Minas, to the staple's store which was a crappy oh store, floors were bad laugh out loud, we worked at Greenwood, and in the Giant Tiger, i was good doing the mirror's laugh out loud Joey would say, oh we had lots of fun, we picked apples we painted we did it all i helped Joey on his cars, and i have to say Amanda does great cooking, i stayed with them lots, the meals were wonderful, we all had a great oh time, we went fishing, i got lost but found my way, Joey will never forget that laugh out loud, and i was always losing phones, me and phones don't get along laugh out loud, Joey and Amanda's dogs, they always like to see me Browny and Brudes well enough of this, i could go on and on laugh out loud.

CHAPTER 3

About Country Songs

still Mon 14th

Well here playing my songs, they're playing good country songs, the good oh country. Well this nice man Joe Felix i always liked working for him, he is a nice man, and tomorrow should be a good day, and that will be fine. My Daddy is gone, he passed and good man, he worked all his life in the woods pretty much, he was good in the woods cutting trees, to make money to put food on the table, for all of us kids. We were only small, but he looked after us, my Daddy picked apples, he did all kinds of work in his time, my Daddy Charley is his name, i miss him so, he was 80 around there anyway, i wish he was still around but we all go one day, we say we meet again i believe that i really do, and Daddy liked the good oh songs, the country songs and we are just a bunch of country boys and girls, i like the way he would dance and clap his hands under his legs, he would do it so cool. Well i am home here at my desk tonight, and a cold night it is Feb 14th now and year still 2020, and i am looking out the window thinking and i see sometimes someone walking, I am in a trailer park, so hard to tell who is walking by, but it is nice to see someone walking through you know, and a friend of yours, that feels nice inside you, and i like helping people that are hurting or feeling pain, i try the best i can of talking to them, and seems to help some, and i feel great about that, and helps them on their way. The day is Sunday Feb 16th well i want to say what has happened in my life through the years, well i have drank booze when i was real young way back i was about 13 even younger i got in it, and as i got older i was still drinking, way up until 200,00 and 6 around that year i know i needed help, i was drinking heavy, everyday if i could get it, it was bad that i couldn't stop not on my own, so i did do a lot of praying asking Jesus for help to get me to stop drinking, cause i didn't want to drink all my life, i would never have anything if i kept on, and you know after i went to God everything got better, i got so i didn't want it anymore, and slowly it wasn't in me to drink, and i was doing okay, i was getting by without it, so if you or anyone needs help with anything, just pray try it and ask Jesus to help you what ever could be wrong, he helped me about smoking, i had a hard time with that to, but i prayed on that, now smoke free with me, God is good and he is love and he loves you to, me and Joey we used to pick those oh fiddleheads, Amanda too we try to make money, and we done good at times, and some times not laugh out loud, but it was fun and falling into brooks, well all in a days work laugh out loud, well Joey you and Amanda are in my book, that is something you want to keep, and the dogs they like me.

Chapter 4

Me and My Friends

Tue 15th

Well got back to my desk, i was doing a lot of painting tonight, i was painting my home, a lot of things i was doing, and my brother David he just came in, he wanted my help, i got back home, he works to picking apples, and i like to get down to see my sister Shirley, or she may get up, it is not far from where she lives, i can ride my bike to see her, i ride to Greenwood Mall on my bike, so it is not to far, i go to see what i may want or need, if i need more paper or notepad, things to write on, then i would get so i can write, and sometimes i visit Janet just down from me a bit, she is a great friend and she is nice, she is a believer in Jesus and that is good, i believe to, and I love going to church when i can, sometimes work takes me from it, but i do go to church when i can. And i want to this Sunday, this is Fri 14th so Sunday i want to be in church. Well i got down to visit my sister today she loved that, we chatted some, and i talked to Henry her husband he was relaxing he liked that, so after chatting, it was still nice out, so i went home i was getting sleepy, so went home to rest. I was to the Mall today, i go there a lot to play the piano and i am getting better on that, and i like playing piano, i pick up on anything and sing feels great, and a woman that works in Giant Tiger, i talk to her i said about the book i was writing, and she would see me come in and say how is the book, i would say well not to bad be a little longer yet, and she wishes me good luck everywhere she saw me great woman.

Chapter 5

A Little of Me and Where I Worked for My Daddy

Well here i am in my bedroom, my desk is where i write, and think by the window, i have painted some more getting things done, it looks good. I have worked for my Daddy when he was living, that was way back in years, i made some money and i piled wood for him, and piled wood 8 feet long 4 feet high i think, it was to make a cord, i made some money and i think 50 to a 100,00 dollars, but things were cheap then, 50 dollars would go along ways, that was a long time ago, i wasn't that old, in my teens 13 or 14. Well not much going on tonight, well i think i will get ready for bed, i have friends next door, Tom and Patsy, and see their grandkids, they are great people, they are great friends to me, i get Tom to take me to the stores when i need to go, very good friends. Well we used to live in Morden, and that was a long time ago, i wasn't that old there, i used to live there with nanny and uncle Leo and Ralph he was a good friend to me, i used to talk to Ralph when i was hurting, he would say it be okay Lar, cause he would call me Lar, i would say thanks Ralph, that was nice, i feel better already, and he would say see I know, and Ralph he passed now, but it would always feel good, after i have talked to him, and i do miss him so.

Chapter 6

Pretty White Snow

Oct 2019 Wed 16th

At my desk writing, looking out my window, and seeing the pretty leaves, where they have changed color, and look so pretty they really do. The winter is getting closer and cold, and soon will see that pretty snow again. When we were just kids, and it was fun, and we would have sleds and go sledding down the hills. Oh we all thought that was great, and having a good time, having lots of fun. Well now you don't see much of that anymore, you may see some kids out playing in the snow. Well i am saying this goes back along way in the years, don't know right on top of my mind, but i can remember us, and everything was in black and white. The old tube TVs the old radios i can remember, and i wasn't that old 10 or11 i would say, so that was far back. Well some of us were old enough to help momma with things, and we done a lot of that, and was happy and glad to help momma do her work. I liked it back in those years, and when Christmas came every year, and we would have the real Christmas trees and the great smell of the trees. I sure loved those days, now it is not the same, you don't see that many people that have Christmas in that way like it used to be. Well now days it is hard and money wise, you just can't, the time and all that changed now, but makes you sad when you think about it. We like to have those times back again, but it is the way it is, and we keep moving on. I believe those times is when i learned to play guitar, well me i can pick up on anything like piano all that stuff, guitar and mouth organs, anything i would say, i call these days the good ol days.

CHAPTER 7

I Live Here in A Trailer Park and More About My Sister Shirley

Well looking out my window, no one comes here too much, and i am mostly here alone, but it gives me more time to write. Well home here in the trailer park, seems like a still night again, not that cold outside, but saying rain for tomorrow, but it could change. Back to my sister Shirley, she said she will come up to see how i am doing, and we talked about things back in the past, it was good things we talked about the good oh times we had back then. Now time just flies by, but i go out to see some of my friends, gives me something to do when i have free days. Well we talk about this and that, we laugh, we go through things, we lose loved ones, but things happen, we never forget our loss, they are always with us. Well here at my desk today, and it looks like a great day, a little cold but not too bad, soon be getting warmer, and i can get out more to see friends, still 2020, and i think i will go to the Mall. This is another night and not too much going on right now, and dark out, and here with my radio on and good songs, but may hit the sack, cause a little sleepy, and may take a rest. Sunday 23 third the other day i was at my brothers place Ronnie not far down the road, and we had a great loving time, i got playing pool, and i got into singing, they say i am a good guitar player. Well i went to my sister Shirley and Henry's. Shirley was out for a little bit, so i waited with Henry he showed me down stairs, he showed me his stereo set up and things likes bikes and a few more things, me and my brother-in-law Henry.

CHAPTER 8

Got My Friends Wood in Joe Felix and More About My Sister Shirley and Her Husband Henry

I have a stand i have found, it was out by the roadside, it was put out, they didn't want it, so i thought it would be good for me, that i could use it, the stand looks good. I got my friend's wood in now Joe Felix so it is undercover, i haven gotten down to my sister Shirley yet and her husband, but i will. It is not bad tonight, it rained some, well soon be dark out, i am at my bedroom at my desk again, at the Mall, they have a piano there, i go and play it some and anyone can play it, i have a piano or i did, it was to big for the trailer. Well my older brother Everett we had good times, and we end up living together he was going through things rough i have talked to him a lot to comfort him, after a break up of his wife, he was not good, and i would know, cause where he was living with me, the things he said, but i won't write that all in the book, i wouldn't want his wife Faye blame herself, they couldn't live together the way things were going on and i would want Faye to know Jesus forgives and he loves her and wants her to go too him he will forgive her, and i believe Everett went to Jesus to, well i could say, we all went through the hard times no matter what, that is if you want to forget what you go through, but some people can't or don't want to, they carry it to their death, and that is what my brother Everett did. Remember Faye don't feel bad about it okay you can't blame yourself, go to Jesus and i love you i want to see you in heaven. Everrett was about 60, maybe older it was 200,000 and 6, it seems it wasn't that long ago, time goes fast it doesn't wait. My momma she would wash clothes back in those times, back in the 60s i would say, and she would have a tub or something to wash our clothes into, and dry them on the outside clothesline she would have geared up, and when i got a little older she would get me to help putting the pole up, and she would have a nail on the top of it to hook on the clothesline, and she would get me to pouch the pole up until the line was up high from the ground, i always helped momma, well the other boys were out somewhere, or a bit too young to do much, i was older than them, so i could help more and glad to do it back in those days.

Chapter 9

It Should Be A Great Sunny Day

Time 16 after 9 PM, well soon get ready for bed, see what tomorrow will bring, it should be a great sunny day, well it is another wonderful day, i am home now, was on my computer checking things out, see if i had any messages. Well i should get ready for bed, and don't know what i be doing tomorrow. Write, i guess, when have free time, and i like writing, i really do, keeps me busy anyway, i think i will call it a day.

CHAPTER 10

Well I Sent to All of the Family Saying Thanksgiving to them

Well i sent to all of the family saying thanksgiving to them, my sister Lois she had 4 girls, i sent them all a happy thanksgiving to Jodi, Krystal, Tena, Laura, my sisters girls, i love them all the 4 girls, whatever they go through i try helping them get over whatever they go through if hurts pain broken hearts i am here for them, and they know that, we all go through something and we all need help from time to time. Well my brother Ronnie, he works on cars, peoples cars trucks, whatever he does, and gets paid for his work, and he likes doing it, i have to get down and see him, i get busy but i have to start visiting more, i know he would like that. Well my friends Tom Patsy, i go over to see them a lot, they are nice friends, Tom takes me to stores when i need to go, and i pay him, he likes coffee so i get coffee, i ask them to come over at times, and they come, i make them coffee, they are very good friends. This still 2020

Fri 21 first, well home here tonight at my desk doing more typing, and i got into my singing again, cause one day i have put it all down for so long, never got at it for along time, and didn't really care if i sang or not, but believe this, that i believe that Jesus brought it all back again and i feel great, well i go through things and life takes it away, and i just didn't feel to want to sing and play guitar, but now i do and want to stay in it, cause i do sing in church i like church, and Jesus is in my life, and he can be in yours, if you just repent and ask for forgiveness of your sins, and he will come into your life, and you start living for him, it is a great feeling.

CHAPTER 11

My Sister Shirley's Husband Henry I Worked for Him

25 after 10 PM. Well me and Henry, he worked in the woods, i used to pile wood and other things for him, they say i was a great worker, and i was, i had to have everything just right when i used to pile wood, i was good at it, i never used a power saw much, but my brothers were good of cutting trees down, and my Daddy, they were all good with a power saw, and me i just mostly pile for them, and they would pay me, that was way in years, way before the year 200,000 hit, i was only young then about 12 or 13 something like that i think, but i liked it in the woods but so much for that. Things never cost that much in those days, bags of chips never cost much or candy, but how it changed through the years. Momma used to sew our clothes back then, and she was good at that, and i visit family more we all have great times, we all grown up now, and we still look out for each other, if one is hurt in some way, we

were always like that we are loving people, and like to help others if they need help. Well i go to Ronnie's a lot, we have great times there and i help him with things there sometimes, and he fixes cars for people and gets paid for it, and that is good. And i go to Shirley and Henry's, i sing and i made up a song for him and burned a DVD too to keep, he liked that, but i hope he gets to read one of my books, if things go well, and the books get out.

CHAPTER 12

About Me Where I Worked on My House

Well not working today, so at home working on my place, worked in my bathroom to get it looking good, and other places in my trailer, i have been doing painting in the living room on the walls, bathroom wall, and bedroom walls, getting things done. Well the sun is out, but been raining, still is i think, cause i hear it, but maybe nice tomorrow, well never went nowhere, still home here, i got done working in the trailer for now, i look out my window, looks like clearing up, and turn out fine that will be good, and that is about me for a while, and i see the nice wonderful trees outside, they are so pretty to see, and no one has come in today yet, so i guess i will take a break, and get back at it, it is 10 after 6 P,M, and i took a load of clothes over to my brother David, to get washed, and in a hour i will go get them, and dry them out at my place, he is trying to fix Lois's computer our sister, so that is what he is doing.

Not nothing going on tonight, just that i have my time writing, don't know if it rains tomorrow, i hope to get to work soon. Well Allen Ronnie and Tammy's son, he is all grown up now making great money driving these great 18 wheeler trucks, and Sandy i still feel i am his uncle, he has a job driving 18 wheeler trucks for Allen, Allen hired him, so he is doing good.

CHAPTER 13

I was to My Friend Today

I am home now, it is night a friend next door came over crying, Bath's girl just a young lady, she was with her kids, and had trouble with one of the older kids, but things are okay now, i tried helping her, i said stop crying what is wrong girl, slow down, she said one of her kids took a fit, hitting her throwing things at her, so she gave me her moms number, but i couldn't get ahold of her, but i tried again and Bath got back and said things are fine, and she thanked me trying to help. The day is Sunday March 15th now and things going good, but this virus is getting around and makes you sick, and can die from it, and i believe it will get in N,S. Well hope i don't get sick or it could be the end of me, but anyway i can't worry about it, i just keep moving on.

Chapter 14

About Family

Oct 20th Sunday

Got on the computer, see if i can fine work, and my mommy she was real nice, i used to help her all the time, as i got older, us kids used to help her get water, when water has frozen up, we would have car hoods, to get water from down over the bank to the brook, the hard times but we did it, those were the olden days, and momma would work hard and a great cook, and we got wood in the house on car hoods to, a great thing to hull wood, and that was in the 60s or 70s. I should of wrote the book the years i was growing up but never thought then, so i just remember that far back and this is 2020, i am writing just in these years now as i go, and think and being alone is the best to write.

Chapter 15

About Me

Here at my desk, i see kids out playing, and it is nice and sunny out today, i never been doing much, i have not been working anywhere yet, but I hope to be soon, and at times i just take my bike and go riding, just to get out, meet some friends. i hope this book does a lot of good for me, and i haven gotten around to visit my family much yet, and they have not been here a lot, busy i guess cause people get busy and don't have the time, but they know i am fine, i was only young, i would babysit my sister Lois's kids, the 4 girls. i think I was 20 younger, i used to smoke then, i would babysit just for a pack of smokes, but now i am 62 but in Feb 13th i be 63 so claiming up, i don't smoke now or drink, and i feel a whole lot better, so i am older now wish i should've thought about writing books then, but never i was so much running around, and at those times i have been drinking and broke a lot, never had money half the time, never saved much, but when i did i would spend it for booze, but now that my life changed, cause i didn't want to drink all my life, cause i know i wouldn't have anything to show for, and now where i am older, i got a thinking, of writing, get into writing books, so hope i am not to late i am going to try hard at it.

Chapter 16

How Bright The Day Is

The time here is 8 after 12 AM, it is a great day, the sun is out, it is wonderful out, i wasn't out yet, but will be, to enjoy the day it won't be to much of these great days, it will turn cold and soon be snow, it is coming winter, the snow be here we will play in it, but guess i am to old for that laugh out loud, but snow is pretty, i know we had lots of fun playing in the snow, when we were kids. We had a great time with friends, i am here in my bedroom with my radio on, good songs playing. I may take a bike ride in this nice day, and now i got back from the bike ride, it is 8;30 PM now, i was over to my friends, Tom and Patsy's for coffee, and got back, and on my computer, see if i got any message, but not to much on. 2020 well i am here today a bit cold but winter is getting over, and soon will be spring again, and work will be out and more jobs to do, and i will be making money again. Well i am looking over to Tom and Patsy's place, sometimes i see their grandkids playing outside. They have fun, and that is good i like carrying on with them a lot.

CHAPTER 17

What We Did Today

Well i did some riding today, it was windy and some rain, i went to Greenwood Mall, just to get out, i do writing in between times, i went over to Tom and Patsy's, tonight had coffee and watched TV with them, it rained hard at times, so other than that, i never did a lot but i was on computer, that was about all. Well home tonight i get paid tomorrow, i need to get some food and stuff, to keep me going, i get lots of food, i go to see friends when nothing much to do, i get Jesus word out, time is getting short, i live for Jesus so i need to do things right, he works within me what to do and what to say, even with family Jesus loves them, i am to move on if Jesus can't get to friends and they want to go there way, even family if they want to stick it out their way and what they think and believe i will still pray for them, and hope they make it to heaven when their number is called, i know i slip my self, but i pick up and go to Jesus again, he won't keep me going to places, where he gets nowhere with people, i am to wipe my feet and move on, that is all i can do and am to do, but i can pray and can't let them get me on a stray of what they think and believe if it is wrong, that will be up to them, i don't want to be left behind when Jesus comes, i want to be good, it will be sad and where they will go, and they know where that is if not right with God, but me i want to be in heaven, and Jesus saying well done, and i would like to see my family there in heaven, if they change and live for Jesus, i will pray for them, and i know things before it happens, if i am real close to Jesus, and Jesus within me knows, cause he uses me, and to get me to know this, so i can help people, if they are not a wear of it.

CHAPTER 18

Went Bike Riding it is A Great Day this is Another Day

Went bike riding, it is a great day, this is another day, i took my camera with me, and took some photos, where i was with my friend, he is some where but don't know right now, but hope he is doing fine, he is a friend of mine, that is all about that, but anyway i miss him even that he is 72 73 years old now, i just miss the times we had, and i may not see him again, it is hard to tell, but he will still be a friend to me, and we are not to hate, i learned that in church, i try talking to him about God and that, so i hope his life changes for the best, cause Jesus loves all, we know we do dumb things, and we have to pay for it, but hope things go good for him.

CHAPTER 19

I Need Money

Fri 26th

Went to the Mall in Greenwood, about a 20 min ride on the bike, i went just for something to do, we still have good days yet, it is going to be cold before to long, it is cold out now, i have my heat on, winter is hitting us soon, it is night here now, 7;51 PM well about money guess we all need money now days, things are getting harder now, and hope things go well that i won't have to worry, that i will come into money one day, i work some but when you do have money it goes fast, but i need enough money banked, if i reach my goal, so this is something i am doing to be a writer, if works out, so i guess it is enough talking about money for now. Another day and i was over to my brothers, he got my computer working, he's down loading windows 7 in it, so it would update, it is working good now, and i took a ride to Greenwood, and got a coffee and i went to work, worked for an hour for a friend made 10 dollars, and he gave me food to get by, until i got my money, i get each month, it was my friend Harley that works at food bank, and i got a Christmas tree from him to from the food bank, so things worked out, when you think they don't GOD BLESS.

Chapter 20

My Brother

Oct Sat 26th

My brother he just came in, my brother David, he borrowed something, and pays me back, i never worry about that, he is a great brother and it is 55 to 11 PM and getting late, i will soon go to bed, and Sandy he came in i am his uncle, this is another day now, we talked me and Sandy, he plays guitar and we play and sing songs, country songs, we have a good time, and today not working, but will be Sat, not to much going on, Sandy he left but we had fun, i am just home and writing, I go out and see these pretty trees, where they changed color, and losing a lot of leaves but pretty.

Chapter 21

Family Time Again

Mon 21 first

I got my bike fixed, my brother David fixed my tire i had a flat, so now i can ride my bike again. Well hope to get work soon now, winter coming to the end, so work should be out be openings for jobs, so that will be good. Well i found work and that is good for me because i like to still work, i am 63 now i slow down a bit, but i like to keep going. It is nice to have outside work because of the fresh air, and that is good. Well my Daddy i miss him so much, and momma, we all do, we did a lot of things for them out of love, my brothers would work on our Daddy's cars, i would help momma what she wanted done, she would get the oh fires going, in winter i would bring wood in and small sticks, to get the fire started, in the stove, i wasn't that old doing that, but i loved helping.

Chapter 22

About Me Today

Tue 29th

I am at Middleton to Tim's coffee shop, waiting for the bus going to Greenwood Mall, to get a few things, that is it for now, and Halloween was last night, the kiddy's were out trick or treating, they were getting lots of candy, i had nothing this year to give out, i had no money. i was sorry about that, but maybe next year, i am here not doing a whole lot it is windy here tonight 5;31 PM it was windy all day but be nice tomorrow i hope, cause i be going to work in the morning.

Chapter 23

Lot's of People at the Mall

Nov 2019

I went to the Mall today, it was a lot of people there at the Mall, i was there on my computer, and i walked around a bit, saw some of my friends there, time goes back tonight, so be early in the mornings getting up, we all need money these coming times now, the way things are, they are costly now, and don't get better less you got money in your pockets, and i hope that happens to me, that i will have money that won't have to worry about anything, and right now i rent, but this whole thing works out for me, then that would be great, wouldn't that be nice, but time will tell and hope for the best.

Chapter 24

Me Finding Work

Nov Tue 5th

Yesterday the 4th i made good because i bought food and a few things, and today i am going to the Mall, i will buy a coffee and go to the dollar store, we have a dollar store here at Mall, so i go to that, and look around sometimes, you get good stuff there, i buy that line cards that you can write on, phone numbers or addresses anything you want to do with them, i am always writing doing something, i write things on the cards good things to have, they are white cards that have the lines in them, and a 100,00 in each package, and i have lots that i won't run out anytime, last me a while laugh out loud, and i still buy them sometimes, they are great cards for my use anyway. I am here looking out the window, facing Tom and Patsy and looks good out really, well guess this is it for this chapter, i know some are short, and i am trying to fine work i need work to pay bills these days, but i will have work, i will fine something anyway, takes money to do things, but things will work out.

Chapter 25

Home Just Typing Working in My Book

Sunday 10th

Well here at home, i see my brother a lot now David, we talk about good things, and i fine work now making a bit of money that i can use for my book i have wrote, and we go for drives and get pop or coffee, it is great, me i like my pop for sure, i drink a lot of it, i still visit Tom and Patsy, and their great grandkids, i still give candy and gum out to them, they love it, so this is it for this chapter, nothing more to fill it out, but guess fine.

Chapter 26

I Visit Friends Next Door Tom and Patsy

I visit Tom and Parsy, watched a movie with them, so now i am home tonight writing, not bad out but we have a storm coming, not far away, into next week it will last, never went to stores tonight, well they were closed anyway, cause remembrance day, but tomorrow they will be open, but haven much money, i want to get Christmas things to put up, i have a tree to put up when it gets close to Christmas, makes it all pretty that will be good i do have free time, i go to church i have a song to sing in church when i get the time to get set up and what Sunday. Well went down to Joe Felix today to help him get his wood in the wood shed, so we got that all done, time now 5 after 6 PM i went to the Mall earlier, and it rained today, and never did much. i worked for Joe Feix every year to pile his wood up, he is a great man to work for. Tom and Patsy, they are so nice i like visiting them, have coffee and their grandkids would come over, i go to see them i play guitar they like my singing, and i like singing, i played guitar now for along time, i started learning to play about 12 or 13 years old, i say that is good.

Chapter 27

The Dark Night

Well this is a dark night, and a very still night, it said snow at midnight, and in the morning, might not be doing nothing tomorrow if it is bad out. Well this is another new day and it is snow and Thu 13th and snow still on ground, but don't think it will stay. Well i am home today this is a new day Fri the 15th, and cold and raining out, but not much to do right now, but right back to Daddy, i do miss him, so enough saying that and i miss Daddy, but we both picked apples together made good money, he was 80 something when he passed, and i get my cheque the 26th i think, and i will get more things i need, well i am home in my living room, and looks like rain, i was going to Kingston, i may yet, i have things to do there, my landlord is fixing a trailer up beside me to rent, he is getting it ready, and that will be nice. Well hoping to get working again i do these small jobs if anyone wants something done, i need the money to get this book out, i get most of the money saved, so need 80 dollars more and i will get that. I got seeing my friends in Kingston i have friends there i see and talk to them chat and that, we have fun and all and i like that, and it is good to have friends.

CHAPTER 28

Seeing Friends Next Door from Me

Fri 15th

Well been next door, Tom and Patsy's, they have their grandkids there, girl there tonight, they know me good, i give them candy once in a while, and they like gum to, i always have it on my table, cause i know they will ask me, i like that, i will say yes i have gum, i would bring some over to them, i am home now, i watch videos on YouTube, i keep busy doing things, keeping my home clean. Well another night, Sunday 17th, well i hurt my foot last night, when we were working, slipped and fell, but next week we will beat it again working, my foot the ankle part is sore, maybe i twist it i don't know but got better, it is dark well not much to do right now, in this is still night, days go fast, but anyway i will rest. It is Tue 19th i am in my bedroom, the bedroom is my office, everything is there laugh out loud, a friend

James came in last night, looking for a guitar string, but i didn't have the one he needed, but he stayed a while and went, sorry i couldn't help him, but he will get a guitar string somewhere he said no worries.

CHAPTER 29

Got Things Up for Christmas

Well i got some Christmas stuff up getting my tree up later, and looks like a rainy day, didn't go anywhere yet, don't know if i will, looks like rain and i did things in the house, and i still have my piano i play on, i get to play it pretty good, and i need to get new strings for my guitar, i make up my own songs, i sing in church, i be singing soon in church. Well this is Nov 25th on Mon, it is raining today, but i have my Christmas tree up, and lights along the windows, looks all pretty, Christmas soon be here, people got their pretty things up, it all looks cool and pretty.

Chapter 30

Getting Things Ready for Christmas

Nov 2019 Sat 30th

Well i was busy the last few days, getting things up for Christmas, my tree is up, and it is all trimmed, got lights all around the windows, got a lot of Christmas things set up in the house, got them sitting everywhere to be seen if people comes in, it is all good and pretty. Snowing here now, and cold out, roads not that good, they are slippery to be driving, so i am not doing to much now, until i get more money to get more Christmas stuff i hope, get some more candy, to fill my stocking. i have some in it now, well the hours are going fast, i had a break and had coffee, and had my dinner, it is going in evening now, and still says snow, but a little better tomorrow i guess, and just had a friend come over a few mins ago, to see my tree, and the things i have up for Christmas, getting colder now. It is almost 3 PM this is Fri now the 6th and it is Dec, i am home watching a movie, and things already for Christmas.

Chapter 31

A Rainy Day

Dec Tue 10th

Well raining out and no work today, Christmas will soon be here now, be lots of fun and i wasn't writing for a while, been working and tired when getting home, but got back to it. Well not much to do, and a rainy day outside, i was over to my friends next door, Tom and Paray's, to see their place, see how they are doing, and my phone is broken and no mins on it, but i am getting a new phone soon as i can, this is Fri now the 13 th i be working tomorrow morning, Sat maybe Sunday to. No work today, it is Sat 14th it is raining out now, and rain tomorrow, well another day not doing much just staying indoors cause raining, well i do some more writing, and i will watch YouTube videos, movies, and some Christmas movies. Well no work today, Sunday 14th now less something comes up for work.

Chapter 32

The Christmas Feeling

Dec 2019. Wed 18th

Well today it is getting real close to Christmas, i got Christmas feeling, saying merry Christmas to anyone i meet, we have snow now, but hope it will be so great, we need snow for Christmas right, i have work on Saturday. If it works out i need money. I just visit my friends Tom and Patsy, and their grandkids, the girls i give them some Christmas candy they like that, and i give their grandkids candy all the time anyway i like doing it. It is Thu 19th now at night, this morning i got my Christmas box the hamper so got my turkey, and not much going on tonight, i am sitting back watching movies, and no work tomorrow i don't think, but i bought more candy, my stocking is full, and candy on the table, so got lots, and not that late, it is 25 after 7 PM so think i will watch another movie. Mon 23 third Tue Christmas eve not long now be Christmas day, have fun on Christmas day, be with friends. We have lots of trees around and looks so pretty, and i had my Christmas, it is Thu 26th we had fun, i still have my tree up yet, i will take it down later, and put the trimmings away, for another year again if Lord's willing, sun is out, but cold today, but tomorrow i go shopping get food and things, and it is Tue 31 first, well Christmas went by, i had a great Christmas, but now my tree is down, and put away for another year, all my trimmings put away so tomorrow will be 2020 a new year.

Chapter 33

It was A Little Windy

Jan 2020

Thu the second, day was okay not bad, it was a little windy, now it is night 20 after 9 PM, so i am just home on computer, not doing much of anything, so think i be soon going to bed, get up early, cause going to Mall in the morning. Well the day is Fri 3third, i was to the Mall, to get my money out of the bank, i had to get a few more things, and not to bad out, it is evening now going on night, i am going away at 4 PM, won't get home for a while, doing something for a friend, well i got done what i was doing anyway, and went home, and i will see what happens tomorrow if i be working or not, i hope good and get things done that will be great. Well i visit Tom and Patsy a lot they are good friends to me, and i like going there, they are fun we chat and talk, and have a great time. Well see later the rest of the day, see what i am going to do, maybe ride my bike, i do ride around a bit looking for things i may want, and to use like lumber to build things, that would be nice, i like building things.

CHAPTER 34

A Good Day

Jan 4th

Well it is nice out a pretty good day, i got out went to the Mall, that is where i always go, and got a few things, and i miss my momma and Daddy, me and Daddy we would get mad at one another but that is nothing, we get over it, and i would do what he wanted me to do, he would send me to the store, could be a mile or 2 but i would do it, i would go and get what he wanted, and momma, i would do things for her, when she wanted things done, i would help her and now Mon the 6th, and night now 53 to 8 PM, and got stuff, i am putting a fence up, around my lawn, cause a friend i know is driving his 4 wheel over it, making it messy, i guess he never knew it would get bad, so i am putting a fence up, they may stop and not much going on just yet, i know the guy didn't mean to mess my lawn, he is a good friend, he is trying not to, that's all, it is a still night, this is Frt 10th, another day, i shoveled my driveway out, we got a bit of snow, makes things pretty and white, and i know you have to watch out when driving, roads gets slippery and icey, don't want to go off the road and get hurt, or maybe killed just be safe, it wasn't just him messing my lawn up, it was others too, they should of known better but i couldn't fine the right and strong stuff for a fence so i just left it, if i stay here longer i may fine something.

Chapter 35

Watch The Roads

Sat 11th

Watch the roads, they may be bad, and tomorrow is going to be freezing rain, won't be good and just drive carefully. Drive safe and it is Mon 14,th now another day, but night 40 to 7 PM, and i am home here, i went to the Mall then went to a friends across from the Mall, don't say his name, he may not like it. if he reads one of my books, so i keep it low, he made coffee and gave me some soaks, which i needed soaks, that came in pretty good, and he gave me a package of hamburger so that was good, and i hope it will be good tomorrow, cause i may go to Kingston, but not far to ride a bike, take about 20 mins or more, i have a great spot i go to, makes me have this great feeling, a wonderful feeling, it is a place close to looking like the Little House On The Prairie the trees almost looks the same, but i call it Pretty Trees On The Hill i go there and sit a while, give me that wonderful feeling, so i found a place i like that, why not use it, not to many knows about it, but i am about to let them know, who knows where it might go. I ask the owner cause I wanted to name it that name i said, and the ones that owns it and said it would be fine, so i put up the title Pretty Trees On The Hill, they say nice, so i can use that spot and sit and rest, drink coffee eat whatever there, and i said to them, cause that spot gives me a feeling, inside me like i could live there forever, if you know what i mean, and i have things in mind about that spot, i like to do something with it, i want to get seats there cause no seats, but i will come up with something down the road a bit, i said can i clean around it in summer, and they said sure, so i will do that, rake clean and keep it nice, Fri 17th now, and i will rest a bit.

Chapter 36

Working on My Spot

Well this is morning now, later on i think i will work on my spot in Kingston, the spot that reminds me of the Little House On The Prairie, i was a loud to name my spot in Kingston, Pretty Trees On The Hill, i like that name, so i believe i be doing that today, i don't know what will become after that, may be nothing or something, it is a place that i feel good being there, a feeling like i can see the kids running down the hill on the Little House On The Prairie, but this is not in Wal Nut Grove laugh out loud, this place i found is here in N,S, in town of Kingston, but the trees up top the hill reminds me, trees something like the trees on Little House On The Prairie i guess that is why i like my spot, and feel good there, well i like it i have my coffee or chips something i will have, just have that great feeling, and i thought big things at my spot, like taking movie shoots with camera, have some sets build for actors, get some people and kids in the movies have it going in seasons summer and winter, for how long the seasons end wouldn't that be cool, but don't think that will happen, but it is in my oh little head to do. Well another night here and i write away, not to much going on, momma was a loving mom, and we all miss her, but we move on until we get there when our number is up, well guess i will pack it in for the night.

CHAPTER 37

About Family Some About Momma

Wed 22 second

Well momma, she was always nice, she brought us up the best she could, we got older and helped her around the house, we were always moving around, i guess that is where i got it from, always moving, my address is 19 Sheffield Dr Kingston N,S, BOP 1RO, now if i stay here and stop moving around laugh out loud, but anyway i hope my book is wonderful to read, and people like it, if gets out i hope, it is my very first time. Back to momma, well she always liked walking i walked with her some, I believe when we lived in Middleton she was coming from a store, and I was with her, i have walked with her helping her carry stuff she had bought, cause she always liked getting things. Far as i can remember, about Daddy and momma, we all lived for what we got, and be happy about it, maybe didn't look like lots, but we were happy of what we had, and said thanks to momma and Daddy and was a lot of love. Well i remember Allen way back when he was only small, my brother Ronnie's son, we had fun him and Venessa they would always want me to come and spend nights, and i would, we all had hard lives but anyway i will move on in the story, we all love one another, and we are getting older and we move on, we just need to be happy and enjoy life, long as we are still here. Allen he came to me when hurting through life, i said you come through Allen, you will be fine, and i had hurting times, falling in love and falling out of love, i got by and get better, cause started getting out, see me i have to be around people, and it forgets what you have way in the deeper thought of your mind, and before you know, you don't hurt anymore that is how it was for me hoped that helped.

CHAPTER 38

Pretty White Snow Everywhere

Well some people hate winter, cause ice and all and cold, and the roads gets bad to drive, but me i like winter, i have no car, so no worries there about driving, and i like seeing snow around, and it is lots here now in NS to me snow is pretty, i look all around, and peoples houses, all snow on roofs, they look so cool and white laugh out loud and pretty, i know they must hate shoveling driveways and that, some don't have time for it, but they need it done cause can't get out, it gets bad i know, and i don't like it a lot, but i do my driveway even that i don't have a car, i shovel mine cause never know who is coming, and they would want to drive in, so that is why i shovel my driveway mostly, and pretty white snow everywhere i see kids playing outside around, they would move right along down hills, down off the banks, they seem like they are having a great time, i know i used to when i was a kid, i had fun sliding down hills, and seems warm out that day, but looks like they like playing in the snow, and this is my last page for this book, so read and enjoy.

[Wote By Larry Willaim Selig]

Printed in the United States
by Baker & Taylor Publisher Services